# More Memories in Verse

*Taking another walk down memory lane*

**Margaret Bowler**

*(Mrs. B)*

BookLeaf
Publishing

Presentation by BookLeaf Publishing
Web: www.bookleafpub.com
E-mail: info@bookleafpub.com

ISBN: 9789363309395
First edition 2024

*to all family and friends for their
encouragement and support*

## Preface...

*Taken from a happy childhood and family*
*life*
*Growing up in Derby.*

*I moved to Skegness in 1960 to help my*
*mother run a private hotel. I met and*
*married my husband in 1980*

# Acknowledgement

*Thanks to my dear husband,
without whose help and patience I wouldn't
be here today.*

# It really is a tragic shame

But what's happened to conversations today?
If you're not a number in somebody's phone
Nobody has anything to say.
If it doesn't plug in or download
Children don't know how to play
It really is sad they are missing so much.
Friendship, sharing and such
We played together in all sorts of weather
and our toys either made or didn't cost much.
I'm glad we belonged to the good old days
But not the ones our parents meant
We made our own; we were never alone
And time with our friends well spent.
We played every day without having to pay
In parks or just in the streets
We would call each other
Decide what to do, then just meet.
We'd be out until dusk feeling safe till we must
Go in cause it was school the next day
We'd be tired, sometimes weary
But never felt teary because we had our own way
We can never repeat how we played in the streets.

Kids today would think we were mad
If we told them to go and play outside
They'd say no.
No electric to be had
How times do change, although it's not strange
It really is quite sad.

# Remembering the games we played

As I sit here in the sun
Hopscotch, marbles, whip and top
We used to have such fun.
Skimming cards we used to get
In bags of tea to collect until we had the set
And then we'd swap if we got two
Another game I bet
I know I've mentioned some before
But they've stayed clear in my mind
We didn't have time to get bored
Lots agree with me, I find.
We'd use our energy up outside
Much to our mothers' glee
They call us in to wash our hands
When it was time for tea.
And then on lighter nights
We'd go out and play again
The only thing that kept us in
Was if it started to rain.
During holidays, we'd go to the park
Where it was free to play
On swings and roundabouts

Sandpits and such, we'd probably spend the day
A sandwich and a drink of pop
Would keep us going till tea.
Our parents never worried
They knew where we would be
We had the freedom way back then
Felt safe while we had fun.
Sitting here, remembering back
Reminded me, sitting in the sun

# The things our mothers used to do

Would be laughed at nowadays
But I love to think back with fondness
To some of her funny ways.
Because I lost so many gloves
She'd stitch them on some tape
And sew them in my sleeves.
It was something I used to hate
Trying to get my coat on
They would get in the way.
I'd always end up with an odd one
I was a clumsy child, she would say
'You'd lose your head if it was loose',
Was another saying I would hear.
But she never used to make a fuss
Nor would she swear
She taught me many useful things.
Baking is my favourite of all
I'd be in the kitchen baking cakes
When my friends used to call
'Are you coming out to play'?
But I would cheerfully shout

'Sorry, can't come out today
But I'll bring you something out'.
My mom would go to the pantry
Say 'Where's all my flour gone'?
'I've been baking again', I'd say
'Shall I put the kettle on'?
Since then I've always liked baking
Trying new things to make
I even got to do things like wedding cakes.
Mum used to make better pastry than me
But she said my sponge was lighter
When I made them to have with tea.
We did lots of things together
She taught me such a lot
Never made it heavy weather
So there's nothing I've forgot.

# Waiting waiting waiting

And I'm not the patient type
To sit here contemplating.
I'm really on a hype
But it's no use getting riled up
For a phone call that will come.
When they get around to it
It's not that important to some.
The place looks like a bomb's gone off
Boxes everywhere
We won't know what we need or not
Until we get there.
Just waiting for the key
So we can get inside and see
But they will take their time, of course.
Not just to annoy me
While I sit here waiting
Drinking numerous cups of tea
Then I daren't leave the phone
While I go to the WC.
So I think I'll go out now
To see some friends for a drink
Having a lovely chat

Won't give me time to think.
I know I said it last time
But it's definitely the last
Moving house is stressful
And Time is moving fast.

# I love the smell of washing

When it's been hanging on the line.
The wind blows out the creases
So very little to iron.
We've really missed a garden
Nowhere to sit in the sun
to have somewhere to entertain
Friends and have some fun.
But soon I'm glad to say
These things we'll have again
Moving to a bungalow
And privacy is the main.
But something else I will enjoy
A little more than that
No more rules this time
So I can have a cat.
Although it means a lot of work
Be worth it in the end
This will be the last move
For our golden years to spend.

# I love the sound of summer

What's that I hear you say
The rustle of the trees in a light breeze
The birds coming out to play
Bees in the flowers
Gathering nectar for hours
So we can have honey for tea.
Not a sound of rain on the window pane
Means the sun has its hat on today
And it's warm for you and for me.
Let's go for a walk to have a nice talk
Not about the weather
Maybe have an ice cream
While we sit and dream
Just happy being together
Maybe plan a short break
What we need to take
For somewhere nice and hot
Or meet up with friends
The list never ends.
Of all the choices we've got

It's so nice to get out
That's what summer is about
Doing things without getting wet
But planning aside, it's only a guide
Because it's only springtime yet.

# I'm just a lonely book

Sitting on a shelf
Although there are some others
I feel all by myself.
I've not had time to make friends
I'm taken out quite often
Apparently, I'm easy to read
My story seems to soften
Even the hardest heart
I've heard when people take me back
And discuss the middle part.
Although there is a lack
Of hearts and flowers because it seems
The hero is a stubborn man
Not designed to fall in love.
But he's not met his match yet
A girl who's really out to get
Her prayers answered from above.
And so it goes both with strong will
To see who wins the day

Not letting him see until
She always gets her way.
The author is in charge, of course
So they don't stand a chance
The end is already written because
It's not a merry dance.
It's mostly about the pride of man
But the lady wants some justice
You must have guessed my name by now
If not, it's Pride and Prejudice.

# Volunteering my time

Is the least that I can do
It's better than trying to say
How much I want to thank you
Because of the work you do
My tumour didn't stand a chance
The treatment I was given
Let it a merry dance.
Research and scans did show
What was the way to go
With a no-brainer condition
It means I'm in remission.
Not many are as lucky as me
So giving my time will be
The way I wish to select
A way lots of money to collect.

# Quite an honour I've been told

For the award I received today
I didn't realise my verses would hold
So much interest in this way.
The poet that has been mentioned
I hadn't heard of before
But now it has got my attention
To read her works some more.
My literary prowess has been acknowledged
Something I didn't know I had
It will help me go forward
And I admit, has made me glad.
What this means for the future
As a poetess, I'm not sure
If it's going to help the sale of my book
I'd better get writing some more.
Thank you for the push I needed
To go ahead with publishing a book
What a good job! I heeded your thoughts
And took a look.
So when the opportunity arose

I went ahead without much hope
To find more enjoyed my prose
Giving me much more scope.
I look forward to comments
If you get my book
Let me know how you feel
But for now, although
I've received this good luck
Everything seems so surreal.

# I remember long ago

When I was in my teens
Feeling quite excited
Because of all my dreams.
Remember I said long ago
Because I'm no longer there
But I am happy to confirm
I have someone to share.
The many hopes and dreams I had
Many of which came true
By putting lots of energy
In things I wanted to do.
I've not always been a dreamer
But my dreams meant I could share
To make most of them come true.
Remember I was there
Maybe you were with me
And we had a lot of fun
Making dreams and wishes
What we were to become
So we could look back and say

Those were the days it's true
What made us what we are today
Is what I believe, do you?

# If you're feeling sad

But you're not sure why
Don't feel bad if you have a little cry.
Tears not only wash our eyes
They wash away our fears
So it never hurts
To shed a few tears.
Search for the reason
To show why you are sad
Finding the answer
Will make you feel glad
Then your tears will probably
Be tears of joy.
There are many ways
For tears that you employ
By now you realise
You're not too sad at all
Because it wasn't sadness
That caused your tears to fall.

# When the tears stop falling

And you realise what you've been told
It's time to start recalling
All the happy memories you hold.
But not to keep going back
It's forward the way for you
Make sure of strength there is no lack
Positivity will see you through.
The support from family and friends
Is precious at these times
And will help you see
Happier things sublime.
Don't refuse any help that's offered
You can always repay
Accept whatever is proffered
Keep it for a later day.
It's not the be-and-end all
You might think so at first
Shock always has a knack of making
You think the worst.
Put faith in what is offered

Treatment improves day by day
Clinical teams will offer
What is right to show you the way.
Work with them by staying strong
And you'll find you can't go wrong.
Good luck, I hope you'll be
Lucky in recovery
Just like me.

# Sitting here feeling terrible

Although it's just a cold
But when you ache from head to foot
It could be the flu, I'm told.
A box of tissues at my side
Do not help to keep me dry
With tears running down my face
But not because I cry.
Then my nose joins in
No need to feel out of joint
It isn't a flipping race you know
If you get my point.
Sucking sweets and lots of drinks
But still, my throat is sore
Doesn't matter how many pills I take
I feel like I did before.
I can't be doing with sitting here
Wallowing in sorrow
I just hope when I've been to bed
I'll feel better tomorrow.

# 'Mum, my feet are cold'

'We'll come down off that rock.'
'I've told you before
You're not allowed to wear a sock'.
'But why are my feet so cold'?
She heard him say again
'My dear one, because you are a penguin'.
Animals don't choose to live where they do
But they'd rather have a habitat
Than live in a zoo.
Although they're well looked after
Their freedom is the best
They learn to live together
And get on with the rest.
Although sometimes for survival
They have to fight another
Usually a rival
Though sometimes it's a brother.
'Survival of the fittest', it's called
To give it a name
Ever since evolution
It's always been the same.
When man fights man
It's called a war

To claim the land they live in
Because those in power get greedy
And not able to forgive.
Animals behave better
When looking after their own
They only fight to claim what is theirs alone.
Man could learn a lot from them
If they stayed on their own shores
It would save the lives of men
Because there'd be no need for wars.

# Living by the sea

On a bank holiday
Is hectic, to say the least.
All roads are blocked
With the crowds as they flock
To the front to have a feast.
Donkey rides and more
Along the seashore
Keep the children happy all day.
It doesn't take much
Ice creams and such
All they want to do is play
While we try to shop
For the things we forgot.
It's not easy because you see
Those in caravans seem to make plans
To shop when they get here.
So the car parks are full
Until there's a lull
Only to find they've sold out of beer.
So holidaymakers hear our plea

Bring your own supplies to the sea
At least enough to start
Then we can get to the shops
Without doing it in hops
And manage to park comfortably.

# I've just finished reading a newspaper

Nothing but doom and gloom
For any cheerful stories
There isn't any room.
It's all about war and fighting
Hatred between countries galore
Nothing about delighting
Does nobody get on anymore?
Someone should tell the leaders
To sit down and talk man-to-man
Then there would be no sad readers
Wondering how it began.
Most of those in high power
Don't listen to what people want
Our patience just gets lower
And fear for those at the front.
Didn't two big wars show
How many lives were lost
They should really know by now

It's far too big a cost.
There'll soon be no future generation
They are killing the one to provide
Without any reasonable explanation
The ones to pass on will have died.
We're taught to love one another
But those in power don't know how
Did they never read the Bible
It's probably too late now.

# Never cared for sewing

Once my mother said
'It's a good job for safety pins
Hot needle and burning thread
Is how you sew my darling
Better give it to me instead'.
She once enrolled us in night school
I wasn't excited at all
But I did make a dress and coat
For a wedding in the fall.
I didn't like the teacher
She used to make me squirm
Nothing seemed to please her
So I left at the end of the term.
Now knitting I've got a yen for
And toys, my favourite thing
I really love the knitting
That isn't hard at all.
But putting them together
Is not my wherewithal
Sometimes it is a struggle

I seem all fingers and thumbs
And get into a muddle.
But eventually out it comes
It's because the sewing
Still baffles me, no end
So sometimes I call on the help of a friend.
My mother was right all those years ago
Hot needle and burning thread
I don't think it's my thing to be able to sew
I'll stick to knitting instead.

# Who was your favourite teacher

Not necessarily a name
More a favourite subject
And in each school the same.
I started in the infants
Preferring math the most
Then also in the juniors
A very important host.
Then up in the seniors
I thought it might be best
To help with jobs as well as home
For shopping and the rest.
But by then I'd changed my mind
Because I loved English now
I've always been good at spelling
And that's helping me somehow.
I graduated from grammar school
But didn't like it much
All the pomp and ceremony
Gowns, mortarboards and such

Didn't mean a lot though
I just missed friends so much.
I didn't get any GCEs
By then my interest had waned
I was wanting to leave school and be a nurse
So couldn't see anything I gained.
Alas! A breakdown after two years
Stopped what I'd always wanted to be
I didn't want to pass on my fears
So decided it wasn't for me.
I did other things over the years
But finished my working life
As a practice manager for thirty-four years
As well as being a wife.
I never had a favourite teacher
But one that I really feared
She was a bully and didn't like me
Her lessons I used to dread.
I often got a wrap on the knuckles
And a clip around the head
Until one day a friend told my mum
Who went to see her to complain.
My mum could be a force to reckon with
And she never did it again.
I mostly enjoyed my school life
And got on reasonably well
I got the gift of writing verse
As you can probably tell.

# Two witches sat around a cauldron

Each trying to outspell the other
I'll try to cast a spell on all toads
As they try to cross roads
Then cars will slip on the mess
What would you like to confess?
I'll put a spell on all schools
For turning out many fools
Who work for the country it seems
Can you beat that in your dreams!
I'll put a spell on all wars simply because
The idiots who start them are all mad.
I don't think the above needs our spells
They seem to manage quite well.
On their own, they say it is life
So we can keep all our spells
They will carry on just as well
To cause lots of trouble and strife.

# Boo! said the ghost

'Boo', said the ghost
'Boo to you', said his mate
If there's one thing I can't stand
It's that and all the other daft things
We're supposed to say.
Who thinks these things up
And why do they scare
Just because we can't be seen
And maybe move the odd chair.
Boy, it's cold in here tonight
Is it me or is it you
First to give a fright
With that silly word, Boo.
I think it might be me
You can have the night off too
Is my white shirt mucky at the back
Can you see it?
I rubbed against the wall
When that woman dashed past me
I do so hate it when they scream like that

All I did was slightly move her hat.
She'd scream a whole lot louder
If I brushed against her face
And why do they scream
When they pay to come to the place.
Oh well, I suppose I'd better get
Back to work and haunt
Because they don't think
They've been scared enough
Unless they wet their drawers.

# Oh, what a joy it is to be

Living well and beside the sea
Sometimes it can be quite fun
And sometimes we even have some sun.
Folks come from far and wide
Just to be beside the seaside
Songs have been written
And tributes made
How happy we are
Walking along the promenade.
Donkeys on the beach giving rides
Funfairs also being beside
There's lots to see and plenty to do
Nature, land, with animals too.
Penny arcades making money galore
Bingo, bars, all along the seashore
Buckets and spades are all the children want
Building sand castles and the odd ice cream
Will find them happy and content.
Fish and chip dinner or a burger will do
And for afters, have a doughnut or two

Back to the stations after a day well spent
Tired but happy and very content.
Oh yes, it's lovely having a day by the sea
But living here is perfect for me.

# Two dogs

Were walking down the street
And one says to the other,
'I'm sick of that cat next door
It does nothing but cause bother.
The other day I saw it
Digging a hole in the lawn
Of course, they'll think it's me',
He added with a yawn.
'What can I do to sort it out
Do you have any ideas'?
The other said with a grin,
'I've been sorting ours out for years.
First, you need to make a mess
When everyone is out
Then leave a part of it in its basket
It's sure to get a clout.
Just do a little bit now and then
It keeps it on its toes
It soon knows it's when it annoys you
And likes to keep a clean nose'.

The other says, 'I'll try that
And let you know how it goes'.
A few days later they were walking
He says, 'I think I've cured the cat
I bit a chunk out of the settee
And left it on her mat.
The owner wasn't happy
And she didn't get any tea
I was asleep on my bed
So they didn't chastise me'.
The moral of this story
Don't always think they are getting on
They can be as crafty as each other.
Don't believe the sad look in the eyes
The one that's usually not in bother
Is the one that's telling lies.

# Have you noticed

Adverts these days
Are no longer jolly and funny
Instead of selling things with a jingle
They're always asking for money.
And if that's not enough
It's about funerals
Showing you one after another
Telling you how easy it is
To get rid of your mother.
Although it's the mother paying herself
Starting a bit at a time
So you can go on enjoying yourself
To attend her funeral will be a crime.
The world is turning upside down
Doom and gloom are all that we hear
No more laughter, just a frown
When we watch TV adverts, I fear.

# Why do you wake up crying

When you know I'm beside you lying
With my arms across your chest
Knowing I love you the best
And will till the day I'm dying.

Was it a dream that awoke you?
Was someone trying to provoke you?
I can help if you tell me why
What it was that made you cry.

Every day we are together
We will ride the stormy weather
My love will see us through
I have enough for two.

Speak to me; tell me why
What it was that made you cry
I hope with all I possess
They were tears of happiness.

# Do you remember cat's cradle

Such fun with a lump of string
It's funny how seeing something
What memories it will bring.
I unwrapped a parcel
And had the string in my hand
Without realising I was doing it
I had the cradle but no one to pass the band.
Another one I thought about
Was a yo-yo; I used to be quite good
Taking the dog for a walk
And swing it like a pendulum would.
Be hard and needed practice
When I sat all alone
And two paper cups and string again
Would make a telephone.
When you think about it
Looking back, it seems
We were quite constructive
And not only in our dreams.
We didn't need expensive toys

To pass an hour or two
Then pass it on to friends
When they came to call for you.
We'd play for hours with all sorts of things
Which they throw away today
Don't know what they are missing
Don't know they seem how to play.

You'll never know how hard it is
For me to say goodbye
As I put my arms around you
Trying hard not to cry.
All these mixed emotions
Running round inside my head
Wondering if there's something else
I really should have said.
One last hug, one last kiss
Will this pain ever stop
But do we really have to go through this
Every time I go to the shop.

# Once in a while

I remember your smile
And the world is alright again.
But then you fade away
What more is there to say?
What can I do to make you remain?
A memory in my heart
Declares we're never apart
So why do I feel this pain?
When I close my eyes at night
I feel everything's alright
But you're gone when I wake again.
I know I had you many years
But that doesn't stop the tears
I didn't want to lose you at all.
You gave me all your love
And I know you watch from up above.
But I still wish you were by my side
Knowing we're together again
Does ease my pain.

So in my heart, you'll stay
Till we meet again one day
And be a family again.

# What it is to know a love

The greatest gift of all
Whether it be in the cradle
Or among friends
You should happen to befall.
A lasting romance can be called
A love affair for sure
Sharing many years together
Learning how to weather
The ups and downs
Without many frowns.
A love lasting forever
What is the secret you might ask
Trust and honesty, make it a task.
If you can learn to love like this
A loving look, a feeling of bliss
You have been granted a life of hope
Knowing you will always cope.
So long as your love is always there
Holding you, showing they care
Be it lover, mother, child or friend

The gift of love will see you
Through to the end.

# Good morning, Captain Magpie

I salute you three times too
I hope you have a nice day
Is your Mrs with you.
Many do not like you
They say you are bad luck
But we have lived across the road
Without having any truck.
There are so many other things
To blame for how we live
But fortune is our making
Good luck is ours to give.
What will be will be it's said
That seems for most it's true
To blame a bird for your bad luck
Hardly seems the thing to do.
Many proverbs and sayings
Are mainly up to you
Don't believe all you read
Rely on what you do.
But I'll keep saluting the magpie

It's more habit than belief
It doesn't hurt to do it
And affords me some relief.

# I'm not a lazy housewife

But two jobs I hate to do
Cleaning the oven is not easy
And I hate ironing too.
Getting down to do the oven
When you're not agile anymore
And if not very careful
End up on the floor.
The ironing is now easy
I pay to have it done
My hubby tried it only once
But put more creases in.
So that was that I'd sooner pay
He didn't find it fun.
The oven is still a difficult chore
We are neither of us fit
To get near enough anymore.
I've had enough of it
I think I'll have to get somebody in.
It bugs me having to pay

But that's what's going to happen
At the end of the day.
Now I can rest quite easy
Knowing the two worst jobs are done
Doing the rest is a doddle
I even find it fun.

# Simple Simon met a pieman

On the road to nowhere
Simon said to the pieman,
'Oi, what you got there'?
'Nothing for you', said the pieman,
'Until your manners get here'.
'No need to get nasty
I just want a pasty.
I suppose you're going to say no'.
'Well', said the pieman,
'You got that right,
I've got nothing for those
Without the magic word'.
'What abracadabra is that
That will get me a pie'?
'No', said the pieman,
'Better give it another try.
I'm willing to stand here all day
Until I hear you say
What your mother

Taught you as a child'.
'Oh', said Simon, 'You mean the rubbish
Before I became wild'.
'Wild you may be,
But you'll get nothing from me,
Good manners do not add to the price'.
'Ok', said Simon, 'But listen good
Because I'll not say it twice'.
'Please, may I have a pie?
Is that what you wanted to hear'.
'Yes, it is, but you're too late
Nothing left on my plate.
Your rudeness put you
At the end of the queue.
So the next time we meet
If you want to keep me sweet
You know exactly
What you have to do'.

# The look of love in his eyes

Is a joy to behold
As he looks at the one he adores
As a man watches his bride unfold
The moment she walks through the doors
As she walks down the aisle
With a beautiful smile.
He knows he has made the right choice
And he knows–they will be so happy
He has every reason to rejoice.
The day was worth waiting for
For everyone to see
They would be together
For eternity.
The vows that they make
Vowing never to forsake
Said surrounded by people they love
With the blessing from God above.
Means the two have become one
With each other to lean on

At the start of a wonderful life
On the day they became man and wife.

# I wonder

I wonder if you'll wake up and say
I wonder if it'll be a good day
I wonder if you're family are well
I wonder if you will read this as well.
I wonder if it will make you think
I wonder if happiness is on the brink
I wonder if peace will come
I wonder if it has for some.
I wonder if you'll read this and say
I wonder why you're thinking this way
I wonder why this came to my mind
I wonder why but I'm being kind.
I wonder why, and I hope you don't mind
I wonder why what answers I'll find
I wonder why I'm thinking this way
I wonder why at the end of the day.
Did you wonder too?
If so, I wonder why?

# It doesn't matter

Where we go or who we see
Memories last and will always be
Safely stored in hearts and minds
To take out and recall at will
All the details you remember still.
It may be a sound or a picture you see
That brings to mind what used to be
And still brings a smile to your face
As you bring to mind what took place.
No one can take your memories away
Whether they be happy or sad
They will last for many a day
Often making you glad.
If it's someone you've lost
Not forgetting the cost
Memories help keep them near.
It might take a while
But you'll look back and smile
As you remember what happened so clear.

Memories are like a book
To take out and look
And keep forever near.
Making you glad
For the good times you've had
Even if you shed a tear.

# It must be my age

Cos when I sit down
There's a funny noise
That makes me frown.
No, it's not what you think!
It's a cracking sound
You didn't think that
I'll be bound.
I've always been noisy
With a creak and a crack
Even in my pram
When laid on my back.
And now that I'm older
There's pain there as well
But at least I'm still here
With a tale to tell.
I love going down memory lane
But sitting in a chair
At least there's no pain
I just keep using my brain.
Oh dear, that's a trial

But I do try using it once in a while
I wake up in the morning
And while in my bed
If everything hurts
It means I'm not dead.
So let's take a walk,
Oh no, I hear you say
Here she goes again!
Now back in my day
We had such fun
You've got to admit
Playing games like tick and hit
Marbles, whips and tops were favourites too.
If you fancied someone
A love letter from you
Then wish you'd not sent it
In case they didn't care
And if they turned around
Pretend you're not there.
Some of the sweets we ate
Oh there were many
Gobstoppers, blackjacks
Four for a penny.
Liquorice and Pontefract cakes
Made your teeth black
Sherbet lemons chewing gum
Cough sweets called Hacks.

The choice was so big
Your pennies went far
And they sat on a shelf
In a lovely big jar.
A four-penny mix was chips
With mushy peas on top
We'd get with free scratchings
From the chip shop.
Saturday morning was pictures
Two films, sometimes more
Cos a man playing an organ
Would rise up out of the floor.
With ice cream at half-time
Or a drink with a straw
Slurping in the corner
Trying to get more.
We were quite cheeky, really
But no harm was done
We were just kids
Having lots and lots of fun.

# How do you eat your egg

Is a question often heard
But doesn't very often mean
One that comes out of a bird.
It's usually the chocolate kind
Do you break it, lick it or what
I don't usually have one now
I leave them for children to eat
Before, I couldn't remember how
To me, it was just a treat.
Do you hide them outside to be found
Children find that such fun
Behind things under hedges
But not in the ground
Watching the children run
To see how many they can get
More than anyone.
Easter is a religious festival too
To mark the resurrection of Christ
But to children, it's a holiday to do

Something they think is nice.
Whatever your choice
It's what you prefer
I think a moment on the lips
Is two inches on the hips
So I think I will defer.

# Do you ever wonder

When the stars come out at night
With them being so bright and gay
Where do they go during the day?
Someone is bound to say
They belong to the galaxy, of course
Is that the Milky Way or am I wrong
I don't understand.
I only know they shine
Like a bright star from our life
When we've lost a family member
A mother or a wife
That shone when here with us
Showing us the way
Lighting up our lives
Even during the day.
So when we look up at night
And see that shining star
We think although I miss you
I know just where you are.
The sky is another mystery

In this world in which we live
Unless you know astrology
No answer can you give.
So we'll carry on and wonder
Where the stars hide in the day
And while we sit and ponder
I still prefer the Milky Way.

# Do you remember

The money before decimals came in?
A tanner, a bob and even a florin we'd say
A farthing, a three-penny bit
Were way back in the day.
A Guinea and half crown
Were considered a lot
A silver three-penny bit
In Christmas pudding you got.
A five-pound note was white and very big
A ten-bob note and pound note
In other words, a quid.
Two hundred and forty pence made a pound
And also a halfpenny was around
One shilling was twelve pennies.
We had pounds, shillings and pence
And some of the names
Didn't seem to make much sense.
We had purses just for coins
Because there were so many
And a wallet for the notes

If you had any.
Most things were paid for in coins
And you often heard the sound
Has anybody please got change
For a pound?
A lot of the elderly struggled
With decimal coins because then
It had been a long time since school
And everything was counted in ten.
Now all the coins are different colours
And shapes you will find
It does, of course, help
Anyone who is blind.

# Mr Squirrel and Mr Fox

Were walking through the forest,
'Good morning, Mr Fox', said Mr Squirrel
'What a lovely day it is'.
'Yes', said Mr Fox, 'Are you
Going my way'?
'I'm sorry', said Mr Squirrel,
'I'm afraid I'm rather busy
I've got to gather lots of nuts,
Enough to feed the family'.
Mr Fox said, 'Yes, I know,
I'm also gathering food
It's really hard work
When you have a large brood.
The forest keeps us well supplied
But it needs to be kept inside.
I've just taken possession of an old oak tree
That's where for winter we will be'.
Mr Squirrel said, 'Yes, I've just built a drey
A friend came to help,
But now he's gone away.

We sometimes share,
But this year we are alone.
I've a big family too,
So we need a bigger zone.
Well, I'd best be on my way;
There's not much left of the day.
Good luck to you, my friend,
We'll probably meet again'.
'And to you, too', said Mr Fox,
'Yes, I'm sure another day
The forest is so big,
But I often come this way'.
And so they went their separate ways
To gather food to store
In case it was a hard winter
And they couldn't get out anymore.

# I am a little spider

Incy is my name
I'm sick of climbing spouts
I'd sooner play a game.
I hide myself in corners,
Then when someone's to come about
I run across the floor sometimes
And make folks scream and shout.
I don't know why they're scared of me
I'm harmless and I'm cute
Some must also think I am scary
Because they stand there mute.
I do wish they'd stop washing me
Swilling me down a drain
It only means I've got to climb
Up the flipping thing again.
If you really don't like me
Just put me in a jar
Take me in the garden
Although I won't go far.
Then we can still play silly games

I run, you scream, I hide
So really just to save me time
Please leave me inside.

# What are you like

At growing plants
I'm afraid in our house
They don't stand a chance.
A swamp or a desert is usually the way
I forget if I've remembered
To water them today.
I've not got green fingers
It's obvious to all
You'll see for yourself
If you come to call.
I'm not bad with cacti
As they take no keeping
I'm sure that they grow
While I am sleeping.
I once had a bonsai
And they are a tree
But it didn't stand a chance
Living with me.
I've read all the books
And the card with the plant
But nothing sinks in, my brain, I mean.

I love to see them
But they always seem
To hate living with me
And I'm not being mean.
I wouldn't either if I were a plant
Life expectancy is quite scant
So the one thing not to buy me
Is a lovely houseplant.

# Don't give up on me

I'm still there
I need to know that you still care.
I know it's hard
I don't mean to make you cry
Even I sit and wonder why.
Remember when you kept
Asking again and again
I didn't lose patience
Well, maybe only now and then.
I'm trapped inside
With a brain that has gone
I don't mean to keep going
On and on.
Shouting doesn't help
Oh why can't you see
I'm not a stranger
I am still me.
I gave you all the love I had
If I don't remember you
Please don't be sad.

I've stood by you
So I hope you'll agree
Now it's your turn
To stand by me.
I would have said all this
Before I became unwell
It's only now I'm unable to tell.
You know how much
You still mean to me
I know I can now difficult be.
I gave you life
So I hope you'll repay
Until it's time
For me to go away.
The illness is cruel
But I'm still the same
Forgive me if
I can't remember your name.
We have happy memories
I'm sure you'll agree
We made them together
When I was me.

www.ingramcontent.com/pod-product-compliance
Lightning Source LLC
LaVergne TN
LVHW011050200726
843509LV00011B/1379